Pray
without
ceasing

Other Books by Geoffrey Lilburne
published by Coventry Press

Joy Interrupted: A Memoir of Depression and Prayer

A LIFE OF PRAYER

Pray
without
ceasing

GEOFFREY LILBURNE

COVENTRY
PRESS

Published in Australia by
Coventry Press
33 Scoresby Road
Bayswater VIC 3153

ISBN 9781922589118

Catalogue-in-Publication entry is available from the National Library of Australia http://catalogue.nla.gov.au

Cover design by Ian James – www.jgd.com.au
Text design by Coventry Press
Set in Fontin

Printed in Australia

Contents

Memoir

1

Why Write about Prayer?

I am not very good at prayer. I need to start here for to write about prayer might seem to suggest a particular holiness or spiritual virtuosity on my part, both of which would be false. I am, by nature, a practical atheist insofar as, if I see a problem, I try to fix it *by myself*, and don't first think it should be a matter for *divine* intervention. I don't automatically see God at work all over the place, as some do. I remember my older daughter once remarking 'I'd rather ask a policeman than God for help!' Of course, both she and I have realised that policemen don't hold the key to many issues, and the recourse to prayer has become more frequent for each of us as life's mysteries have unfolded. I see myself as a beginner in the art of prayer and by urging others to pray without ceasing I wish to make it clear that I think this is a pursuit worthy of a life's devotion.

As I look back on my long and interesting life, I ask myself, 'What was it all about?' Does it add up to anything, finally? And if so, what? While prayer is not my natural habitat, I describe mine as a 'life of prayer' because the thing I've persisted in over my adult life has been prayer. I persisted because I regard my 'practical atheism' as a failure of imagination, rather than a key to the nature of reality or a short-coming of belief. It is an imagination that needs to be activated and exercised,[1] and prayer is one of the obvious ways of doing that, as is worship and biblical study. The arguments for atheism always seemed to me weak and their proponents superficial. Of course, living in this age of science, my imagination – like that of so many of my peers has been peculiarly stunted by a focus on the empirical rather than the intuited, the mechanical rather than the teleological. The failure to ask ultimate questions, touted a virtue in some circles, always seemed to me a failure of nerve, just when nerve was needed.

The issue of persisting in prayer will also become a theme in my narrative, so that Paul's injunction to 'pray without ceasing' seems particularly pertinent. It is too easy, in this materialistic and atheistic age, simply to give up on prayer. At times, it seems pointless, and there are many other good things to do. I am dismayed to see how many of my clergy friends have given up the practice as they go about their ministry, and I must say my own practice has at times seriously lagged. The theologically sophisticated may think that they are 'beyond' prayer, but I fear the 'beyond' into which they have moved is a subtle form of idolatry, in which they have substituted something else, perhaps even themselves, for the one true God. Among all the good things

---

[1] For a comprehensive account of how this impoverishment of imagination has occurred in our history and the development of a largely 'god-less' culture, see Charles Taylor, *A Secular Age*, (Cambridge and London: The Belknap Press of Harvard University Press, 2007). My discussion of prayer may be seen as responding to one personal aspect of the great shift in world-view which Taylor so wonderfully explicates.

that we do in our lives, the moments of quietness in the divine presence actually acquire a special value as we ponder life's deepest mysteries. There is a journey here to which we are all invited.

Of course, others have trodden this pathway, and as I outline my journey into prayer I want to call upon a few companions along the way. St John of the Cross has become an inspiration for me, and recently I have discovered the writings of St Teresa of Avila. Later in this account, I will draw upon the wisdom of an American friend, Dr Roberta Bondi, whose journey into prayer has been guided by the desert Mothers and Fathers. As I tell of my travels with prayer, it will be helpful at some points to reflect on how our discussion is illuminated by these accounts of others' experiences and struggles with their own prayer.

It might seem logical to begin this discussion with a definition of prayer – to get things straight at the outset. But that presupposes that one has a ready definition to hand, which I do not. It seems to me that the only way to write about prayer is to write out of one's experience, which seems to be the way all the best writers actually go about it. What has prayer been in my life, in my experiences of its highs and lows? It is perhaps more honest to begin here and then to move towards a definition of what prayer really might be, emerging from first- hand experience. There is no 'theory' of prayer to which we can defer! It is helpful to be reminded by Paul that we don't know how to pray, and it is only with the Spirit's help that we are enabled, and that it is really the Spirit who prays in us 'with sighs too deep for words'. If that is so, then definitions in advance of the actual experience of the Spirit would be pointless.

2

Beginnings:
Prayer as Discipline

My first entry into prayer occurred following my teenage conversion when I gave my life to the Lord Jesus. My heart was aglow with a new warmth and naturally I wanted more, I wanted more of Jesus. I was encouraged to develop a 'prayer life'. What was that? Apparently, it involved regular quiet times, when I would sit in my room with my Bible and, after reading, say prayers to God. Now this was not easy for a young energetic boy drawn to outdoor activities, but I gave it a try. At first it seemed a joy but soon it became a bit of a chore. There were all sorts of 'helps'. There were Bible reading guides offering a daily reading for a whole year, and notes to help you understand and reflect on what you had read. So far so good. It was all new.

But what was I to pray about? What should I be asking God for? Well, in fact, there were all sorts of things and all manner of people. The trick was to make a list and to pray your way through the *list*, rather as Catholics are encouraged to 'pray the Rosary'. So here came a 'prayer diary' in which you split all these multiple needs into the days of the week, and you prayed through them.[2] Prayer was not a haphazard thing that you did when you felt like it, it was a discipline that you entered into, and was to become a regular habit.

I don't know if I expected results from my prayers, although I did pray a lot for my parents that they would come to see the light of Christ. I didn't discern much difference in them as the weeks and months passed! Perhaps I was a bit like Jayber Crow in Wendell Berry's novel of the same name.[3]

> He said, 'What have you got in mind?'
>
> 'Well,' I said, 'I've got a lot of questions'.
>
> He said, 'Perhaps you would like to say what they are?'
>
> 'Well, for instance', I said 'If Jesus said for us to love our enemies – and he did say that, didn't he? – how can it ever be right to kill our enemies? And if he said not to pray in public, how come we're all the time praying in public? And if Jesus' own prayer in the garden wasn't granted, what is there for us to pray, except 'thy will be done' which there's no use in praying because it will be done anyhow?'... suppose you prayed for something and

---

2 See John Baillie, *A Diary of Private Prayer* (London: Oxford University Press, 1936, 53) for a good example of a regular monthly outline of daily prayers for morning and evening. Such a work provided a basic outline which one was encouraged to personalise with one's own particular concerns and persons.

3 Wendell Berry, *Jayber Crow, Barber of Port William Membership, as Written by Himself: A Novel by Wendell Berry* (Berkeley CA: Counterpoint, 2000). This wonderful novel is really an evocation of heaven as seen in a very earthly community in Kentucky, dear to Berry's own heart.

you got it, how do you know how you got it? How
do you know you didn't get it because you were
going to get it whether you prayed for it or not?
So how do you know it does any good to pray?
You would need proof, wouldn't you?'

He shook his head. We looked at each other.

He said, 'Do you have any answers?'

'No', I said...

Like Jayber, in my earliest prayer, I thought it was mainly
about asking God to do things. I thought of prayer as *praying
for*. But at least I knew that outcomes were not the measure
of prayer and that one prayed primarily because it was a part
of the life of faith. My conversion into a rather strict and
rigorous form of Christian discipleship offered me a vision of
prayer as a discipline that needed no justification, no result
or outcome, except what it accomplished in the heart and life
of the one praying.

Naturally, one was encouraged to think of other aspects of
prayer: praise, thanksgiving and confession. Of the latter, I had
plenty, for I was often convicted of my sinfulness. Frequently, I
received criticism from my parents that I was too self-centred,
which often involved my desire to study after dinner rather
than to spend time with them. I felt convicted about this,
confessed it in my prayers, and sought to make amends.

The other constant sins were sexual. Girls were out of
reach, but having discovered the possibility of self-stimulation,
like other adolescent boys, I found other outlets for my
insistent sexual desires. I was convinced that Jesus offered
me the way of victory over this sin, and entered a years-long

struggle to come to terms with my sexual nature. Confession and seeking the Lord's power here became a fairly constant element of my prayer.

It wasn't until my 19th year that I came to see how restrictive and limiting was my type of Christianity. After a year of living closer to my peers in a university residential college, I began to long for a free-er lifestyle and the opportunity to experience spontaneity and self-expression once again. At about this time, I received some more helpful insight into my sexuality, which also contributed to a freeing up of my sense of myself as a child of God. I learnt that my actions and practices were entirely normal and healthy, and not something I had to punish myself about. It was not sinful to be the way I was.

Another form of prayer was, of course, the 'prayer meeting'. This involved a group of folk, usually other boys and a leader, who gathered together to pray for an upcoming event, or for other members of the group, especially the wayward ones. For a young man, this gathering offered a new form of intimacy, as deep concerns were shared and voiced in supplication to the Lord. At university, the Christian Union had a regular weekly prayer meeting and soon I was elected to be the 'Prayer Secretary', hosting these gatherings and preparing lists of upcoming events, missionary challenges and other matters calling for prayer. As a leader in corporate prayer, I would gain skills that would come into good use in my later ministry.

As I took up my professional work as a teacher, the daily habit of quiet prayer in my room ceased to have attraction. I discovered that prayer came more naturally to me as I walked, and so began a practice of 'walking prayer' where an evening stroll after dinner became my preferred occasion for a 'quiet time'. Overall, I was coming to a new understanding of my bodily nature and the possibility of involving more of my physical nature in my prayers. Rather than a demon to be fought, it seems that my body was now for me a means of communing with God.

Within a few years then, my prayer life revolved more around evening walks with God than lists of worthy causes. I still had lists in my head, but it seemed that prayer was more about unwinding at the end of a day and seeking the presence of God, for thanksgiving, praise and intercession. I was beginning to move out of the trap of a fixed style or form of prayer, but knew in my heart that I longed for relationship with God. Was this something for which we needed to strive, or was it simply a gift of God?

This early experience of prayer has some resonance with Teresa's image of the garden. For her, the earliest prayer experience is that of seeking water from a deep well, and then carrying it to the garden which the Lord is cultivating in her heart. In this first prayer, much effort is required to draw the water and to carry it to the plot of holy ground. The work required is that of intellect, which at this stage knows little of the delight of the divine presence and the joy of resting there with God. In this stage, water may often come in the form of tears. She writes:

> ... what will he do here who sees that after many days there is nothing but dryness, distaste, vapidness and very little desire to come and

draw water? So little is the desire to do this that if he doesn't recall that doing so serves and gives pleasure to the Lord of the garden, he will abandon everything. It will frequently happen to him that he will even be unable to lift his arms for this work and unable to get a good thought. This discursive work with the intellect is what is meant by fetching water from the well... These labours take their toll... But I have seen clearly that God does not leave one, even in this life, without a large reward; because it is certainly true that one of those hours in which the Lord afterward bestowed on me a taste of himself repaid, it seems to me, all the anguish I suffered in persevering for a long time in prayer.[4]

My beginnings in prayer as discipline has echoes of this first stage of drawing water from a deep well. Teresa describes the next stage as turning the crank of the water wheel and the use of the aqueduct to water the garden. In this stage, the gardener obtains much more water with less labour, and he can rest without having to work constantly. In this stage, prayer is occasioned with much more delight, by receiving a little knowledge of the 'delights of glory'. I think my discovery

---

[4] *Writings of Teresa of Avila: Upper Room Spiritual Classics* selected, edited and introduced by Keith Beasley-Topliffe (Nashville: Upper Room Books, 1997), pp. 15, 16.

of greater relaxation in prayer in some ways mirrors this stage. However, I do not wish to suggest that I saw a great deal of glory in my life.

For me, the other element of these early years of adulthood was a struggle with mental distress, and specifically anxiety and depression. At this stage of my life, I did not see my acute social anxiety as a real problem until it delivered me over into depression. It is out of the linkage of my prayers with depression that I really began my reflection on the Holy Spirit.

Depression and the Holy Spirit

I have written at length about my struggle with depression in another place,[5] so I will not repeat here what is detailed there. Rather, my interest now is on the intersection of this journey with prayer and the work of the Holy Spirit. It is only natural that one who is afflicted with some kind of emotional disturbance will seek the solace of prayer. Indeed, if you have no awareness of the treatment of mental illness, you first think that the problem is purely your own and you seek to bring to bear what resources you can muster. In my own case, following my religious conversion, it naturally became the subject of my prayers.

---

[5] Geoffrey Lilburne, *Joy Interrupted: A Memoir of Depression and Prayer* (Bayswater, Vic; Coventry Press, 2018). The present work is a companion piece to this book, fulfilling the second part of the title to reflect more fully on prayer.

Indeed, for one growing up in a pre-therapy context, mental afflictions may well be considered as weakness or moral failure. The religious person – and a great many non-religious – will turn first to God for help. Perhaps this affliction is evidence, if further were needed, of one's sinful nature. In my case, I resolved to seek the help of God to overcome this personal failing. I even kept a record of my struggle in a journal that I commenced in my 19th year. Prayer and depression became intimately linked in my experience, and the journal records the details of my struggle.

But why the Holy Spirit? There are some very good theological reasons to link prayer with the Holy Spirit. Paul writes:

> Likewise the Spirit helps us in our weakness; for we do not know how to pray as we ought, but that very Spirit intercedes with sighs too deep for words. And God who searches the heart, knows what is the mind of the Spirit, because the Spirit intercedes for the saints, according to the will of God. (Romans 8:26-27)

In my case, there was another reason to be thinking of the Holy Spirit. There is a popular strand of Pentecostal teaching that speaks of a 'second blessing' which is available to Christian believers, a 'baptism in the Holy Spirit'. Great claims are made for this blessing and its personal result in certain popular devotional books. I knew I had not had this emotional experience and was persuaded that I was not 'filled with the Spirit'. Confident that if I was filled with the Spirit many of my inner struggles would be resolved, I began to desire this experience.

Like many an earnest soul, I resolutely sought this baptism, in prayer and worship. I wanted the Spirit to overwhelm me and take over my errant life, making me anew in the image of Christ. It seemed a wonderful solution to all my adolescent anxieties. But alas, it didn't come (or perhaps I didn't come!). But something else happened for me. As I read the New Testament, it became clear to me that the Spirit was a free gift, not the outcome of some rigorous effort on the part of a believer. It seems in scripture that it is God's good pleasure to give the Spirit just as a father gives good gifts to his children (Luke 11:11-13). The understanding grew in me that I had already been baptised in the Spirit, and all that was needed was to 'enter into' the fullness of the Spirit.

It may seem that this is splitting hairs, but in my experience it marked a very great change. Entering into what the Spirit has given meant something far different from seeking to have an overwhelming and emotional experience. As a result, when I commenced my first journal in 1962 at the age of 18, I wrote:

> I approach the new year of study and service, renewed in the Lord. Since about second term last year, He has been deepening and enriching my faith. I was at that time fraught with doubts concerning Christian experience and the Holy

Spirit. Gradually, my doubts have been dealt with. Especially at I.V.F. conference were many things cleared up in my mind, i.e.

i) The Holy Spirit may work through what may be termed natural means – e.g. emotional excitement, but he *controls* such things according to his purpose. He is completely Sovereign.

ii) Filling with the Spirit is not something to be strived after. My task it to submit all to his searching and working, and to pray in faith. I now rejoice in the fulness and power of the Spirit.

It was becoming clear to me that in relation to the Spirit, we are in a dynamic relationship that grows and changes over the years. While it was not the case that one overwhelming emotional experience was the key, there was the ongoing need to enter into the fulness of the Spirit daily, to 'stir up the Spirit' in our life of prayer. These understandings gave me a firmer theological and pneumatological foundation from which to seek the grow my discipleship and address the causes of my distress.

It is interesting to me now to note that St John of the Cross worked with a similar set of issues long ago. From a set of foundations very different from mine, he wrote his classic work about the life of prayer in *The Dark Night of the Soul.* Although I didn't know of this work when I experienced my early depressions, I can't help wondering whether John was writing about a similar experience to my own. For this reason, let me now digress from the account of my own experience to consider briefly this work.

In John's view, the human soul desires to ascend to union with God; and prayer is a natural expression of this implanted desire. In this quest, there are times when darkness descends and God seems to disappear. In this state, the soul experiences a loss of joy and motivation to continue in its quest for union with the divine. For John, this state when joy and motivation are lost is not a sign of mental pathology, but simply a stage in the soul's journey. It is in fact an indication that God is continuing to work in the human soul but is now working 'obscurely' or 'in darkness'. The result is the first of the 'dark nights of the soul'.

John's theology and psychology were obviously very different from mine, and that no doubt puts him on another plane to the one I travelled. Growing up in a 'secular' age, it did not occur to me to think that my anxiety and depression were part of God's work in me. Indeed, I felt sure that these issues were 'my' problems, brought on, no doubt, by some weakness or failing on my part. I sought God's help to overcome them but saw these as primarily matters for me to resolve myself! In this respect, perhaps, I was actually my own worst enemy. I seemed to echo unconsciously the kind of bad advice John rails against as 'unwise directors'.

> When God leads anyone along the highest road of obscure contemplation and dryness, such a one will think himself lost; and in this darkness and trouble, distress and temptation, some will be sure to tell him, like the comforters of Job, that his sufferings are the result of melancholy, or of disordered health, or of natural temperament, or,

it may be, of some secret sin for which God has abandoned him. Thus, they multiply the sorrows of this poor soul, for his greatest trial is the knowledge of his own misery.[6]

While our list of symptoms in some ways overlapped, the loss of joy and motivation, the theological interpretations were far apart. I will leave to a later section to discuss ways in which John's insights might inform our own understanding both of prayer and depression.

Love and Other Distractions

My time at university began with me as an earnest student, often found in the library nodding off over some dry history text, like *The Tudors*. In my second year, it dawned on me that I was largely wasting my time in the library, unless it was visiting the basement coffee shop where engagements with young women were readily available. I discovered romance and found that I liked it a great deal. But what effect did this discovery have on my budding prayer life?

My journal indicates that I now had a new source of anxiety, the question of what was appropriate, how far to go in romance without causing harm to the other or indeed to oneself! I began one relationship with an exciting night

---

[6] Prologue, Souls Who Make No Progress, The Ascent of Mount Carmel in *The Mystical Doctrine of St John of the Cross* selected by R. H. J. Sheed (London: Sheed and Ward, 1934), p. 4.

out, only to snuff it off a few weeks later when the Lord told me it was over. Why the Lord wanted it to end wasn't quite revealed; perhaps I grew tired of her, but I think rather it was that my life was full and this was a kind of attraction that seemed more a distraction than the real thing.

Always a late developer, it wasn't until my 21st year that I really developed a real emotional attachment. Finding myself studying opposite a beautiful young woman, I began to offer her rides home from lectures, and soon was seeking to assist her in her own emotional and spiritual struggles. In the course of this, I really 'fell in love' and could not help myself. Anxiety again manifested. Was this galloping relationship 'in accordance with God's will for me, for her?' Together, we prayed as only young lovers can pray, prayers of passion and desire. Nor was prayer my only recourse. I began to visit older friends and seek their advice about my actions and my feelings.

In those days and in those circles, the only way to a sexual relationship was through marriage, so the question was posed. While we were both ready for a physical relationship, marriage seemed a step too far for me. In the end, she left me the following year and soon married another, and, as far as I know, is still with him. Tough luck, young lover, but I prayerfully bore up under my sense of loss and dismay. My faith and my purity were still intact!

The nexus between anxiety and prayer was obviously firmly established from my earliest days. If the note of joy seems to be missing from this account of a prayer life, that is perhaps because with my early episodes of depression, joy seemed to go absent from my life. That is returned later is a story for another place. During this entire time, prayer seemed more of a discipline than a delight, and I was yet to enter into some of the experiences detailed in the accounts of some of the great pray-ers of the Christian tradition. I was clearly no mystic; rather, an anxious young man seeking to live out the calling of a Christian life.

After some rather unsuccessful dating episodes, I met the woman with whom I felt I would share the rest of my life, and we began excitedly to plan for our wedding. To say we came to marriage unprepared and immature would be an understatement. In our early twenties, we fell in love and experienced a strong desire to live together in intimate relationship. The wedding was moved forward to the earliest possible date, and I was confident that once our relationship was set on this basis, the anxieties of my life would dissolve, and I would indeed be 'happily married'.

Once married, however, I experienced a rather severe depression when my unrealistic expectations were not met. My emotional distress interfered with my prayer life. My evening walks with God became solitary times of near despair, as I sought to quieten my heart and find something firm on which to pin my hopes. I had learned by this stage that it was no use praying about the depression, for the expectations that prayer aroused were almost inevitably quashed and the mood seemed only to deepen. I was beginning to learn that introspection and prayer were not the best approaches to this kind of disorder, and that an objectifying presence and insight of another were of much deeper value.

Through these experiences, I came to think of prayer in a new way. Parting company with a litany of requests and needs, it seemed that for the depressed person – and perhaps for others too – prayer became a kind of waiting in hope, a patient exercise that actually needed no words but rather an attitude of the heart, a patience in the presence of God. I now counsel depressed folk not to pray – that is, not to use verbal prayers to God who for them at that moment is largely absent, but rather to rest quietly for a better time to approach God, for the darkness to lift. At these times it is best quietly to accept their mood and to wait in hope for a new dawn to break. John has a similar point to make in his criticism of unwise spiritual directors.

> They do not understand that this is not the time for such acts as frequent general confessions; it is now the day of God's purgation, when they ought to leave him alone, comforting him, indeed, and encouraging him to bear his trials patiently until God shall be pleased to deliver him; for until then, notwithstanding all they may say or do, there can be no relief.[7]

From his very different standpoint, John of the Cross urges patient waiting rather than general confessions. While I do not share John's theology of purgation, I do accept that this

---

[7] St John of the Cross, Prologue, *The Ascent of Mount Carmel*, pp. 4, 5.

change in the nature of prayer goes hand in hand with a changing understanding of the divine presence. I will defer a discussion of this change to a later chapter.

For both John and Teresa, the kinds of attractions I've outlined here would be seen as mere distractions from the higher quest of the soul for God. These attachments would need to be given up as the soul pursued its calling to focus on God and the spiritual ascent. But for a modern person with no ascetic ambition, the search for a partner in life is an essential element of the human quest. How to integrate this kind of affection within a spiritual life of prayer cannot be eschewed or avoided. Yet of course, there is tension in this, and my anxieties over this range of experiences points to the uncertainties I felt as I encountered these new challenges and possibilities.

Journaling and Prayer

In reflecting on my life of prayer, my early journal has been a useful resource. But a journal is more than a record; it is also a part of one's actual prayer. It is often the case that as one reflects on the events of the day or the week or the month, one is moved to transmute the reflection into the words of prayer. Indeed, in the development of a prayer life, times of quiet reflection become part of the actual opening of a life to God. For prayer depends on the ability to develop an inner life and the recourse to words and hope. The intersection of expression and hope is a natural launch pad for prayer.

Perhaps the best way to think about this is to consider the journal as a companion to a record of prayer. For those who are serious about taking up a life of prayer, the use of a journal may be a significant aid and encouragement. We are called to a reflective life and the capacity to write about our lives and to turn our reflection into address to our Lord, to open our whole lives to the divine presence and love is a fundamental move, a doorway to prayer. Not everyone likes to keep a journal, to be sure, but I believe it is an important aid and support for the development of a prayer life.

3

A Journey into Prayer

By 1971, I was ready to undertake a new beginning in life. The early uncertainties of my life had been resolved, and, as a married couple, we moved to the United States to undertake graduate studies in theology and to start our family. I had already entered a wider world with my years of theological study in Melbourne, and now many new horizons opened up for me.

One of the advantages of our life at Yale Divinity School was that I met Henri Nouwen, who was then teaching in the area of spirituality. Although I took no courses with Henri, when I found the stresses of life on a US campus somewhat overwhelming, I sought him out for counsel. After a detailed conversation, Nouwen suggested I take some time out from the stresses of life in the Divinity School at a Trappist Monastery in Spencer, Massachusetts. So, in the middle of winter, I found myself driving up the turnpike to the lovely St Joseph's Cistercian Monastery. Henri felt that the quiet of the place, away from the verbosity of Yale students, might be good for me.[8]

---

[8] For an account of Nouwen's own residence in a Trappist Monastery, see Henri J. M. Nouwen, *The Genesee Diary: Report from a Trappist Monastery,* (Garden City, New York: Doubleday and Company, Inc., 1976).

Greeted at the door by a monk, I was immediately stunned by the beauty of the place and of the life of the monks. Rising early for prayers in the morning, I was transported to a world where a group of men fashioned their entire lives around a pattern of corporate prayer. This pattern of life, which integrated prayer and work, the private and the corporate, was deeply appealing to me. In fact, I found it so aesthetically stimulating, that for several nights I could not sleep!

The prayer here being practised was far removed from my evangelical beginnings. Prayer was now allied with music, and done in a setting at once austere and beautiful. Immediately, I tried on some new forms of waiting before God and enjoyed doing this in company with a body of other devoted pray-ers. A snowstorm buried St Joseph's the following day and I marvelled as the life of the community continued as if nothing had happened. Day after day followed the same ordered progression of prayer in the chapel and in the quiet of one's own room at night. It seemed a pattern that had endured for centuries and would continue forever. But, of course, for me it could not.

I went home and determined to take with me the new forms of prayer I had discovered. Translating my new practices into life back home with my wife and small child proved a challenge, but I persisted. New forms of daily prayer, where the focus was not so much on lists as on a regular repetition of ordered prayers now became the norm. Removed from the setting of the monastery, however, these forms of prayer suffered somewhat, and I began to long for a place where I could practise this form of regular prayer.

Up to this point, prayer had been largely blind to beauty and to place and I had created the space in my own mind to pray. But now the body and place were beginning to intrude into my prayer life. In addition, the aesthetics of prayer had largely replaced the dull discipline.

At about this time, I took up a regular ministry in rural Connecticut. Prayer now became a corporate exercise as I regularly led this small congregation in worship and prayer. A new experience of corporate prayer was opened for me, one that would grow over the years of my professional life. Leading others in prayer is an exercise in prayer but also one of becoming a voice for others in their quest for God.

Contrary to what Jayber Crow surmised, prayer can be much more than 'thy will be done'. Indeed, in praying with people and for people I have learnt to put words to the longings of the human heart. Prayer is an invitation to do just this. In praying alongside others, it is important, I believe, not to translate the desires and needs of the recipient into 'acceptable' or specialised prayer talk, but, as far as possible, to echo the voice the one for whom prayer is being offered. In praying, we do not need to anticipate the divine will or provide God's answer to the prayer. It is enough to articulate the need and the longing of the human heart.

Following my graduation from Yale, I undertook doctoral studies at Emory University in Atlanta, and then, for ten years, became a theological teacher in Ohio. Teaching mid-western United Methodist students in theology for ministry gave me a splendid opportunity to develop my post-Barthian theology in such a way as to preserve what seemed to me the best of my Evangelical faith refashioned to deal with an emerging new world. These were happy, productive years, and, towards the end of this time, I became a passionate environmentalist who drew together his theology and passion for land-care in my first publication, *A Sense of Place: A Christian Theology of the Land.*[9]

At this time, I laid the theological foundations for my later life in ministry. While my theology was open to prayer, I must confess that in this academic phase of my life, my practice of personal prayer lagged far behind my theology. The life of the mind took a major place in my days and spiritual practice was somehow squeezed out. I did, however, maintain the practice of opening classes with prayer, and when I later moved to parish ministry in Australia, I was drawn again into the leadership of corporate prayer for others. In the exercise of pastoral ministry, I took up in earnest again the practice of personal prayer, especially in the times when I turned aside from the busy-ness of parish life to consider its goals and challenges.

While my life moved for a while away from the discipline of prayer, engagement in full-time professional ministry awakened in me the spark that had been lit in my early discipline. With some interruptions, my life-long engagement with the ministry of prayer and leading others in this way has deeply enriched in me the experience of prayer.

---

[9] Geoffrey R. Lilburne, *A Sense of Place: A Christian Theology of the Land* (Nashville: Abingdon Press, 1989).

An Opening to Poetry

From the outset, prayer had been an intensely verbal exercise for me. In the move to engage with the Cistercian prayer life, I began to see the value of silence in the presence of God. But verbal prayer continued to be important and I gradually came to a new expression which was not so much asking for things as expressing to God what was on my heart. In my early Kalgoorlie year, now happily married, I one night penned the following prayer.

> The night is peaceful. Behind a thickening cloud cover, the moon sails in quiet serenity. The countryside rests in peace, receiving with gentleness the touch of rain, and answering the moon's 'Is it well?' with a soft sigh of contentment, gently exhaling the fresh fragrance of rain kissed soil.
>
> A good night's work. And work that is interesting and stimulating.
>
> I thank Thee, Lord, for this evening of calm, and of work. And I thank Thee for the work I may do. (10/4/68)

This prayer has nothing of intercession about it. It is more like the sigh of a soul before God after a day of productive work. Is it a prayer or a poem? Well, perhaps the distinction here would be forced. The environmental description works on its own, but also lays bare the soul that is lifted to God in worship and thanksgiving. Could prayer and poetry be sides of the same, or if not the same, of **similar** practices.

My poetic impulse had first been aroused in the ups and downs of my early love life. I would be embarrassed to share the results of these scribblings! But in time I found a poetic voice expressing itself in a number of settings. After a depressive episode, for example, I found myself writing in these terms.

It comes like the dew overnight.
Next morning it's there,
everything you touch is covered.

Phases of the moon move blood.
Ocean tides creep
into hidden estuaries,
familiar marshlands.
Gently, mysteriously
seepage enters me.

I wake to fear
some sudden
unbidden
descent.[10]

---

[10] Poems cited are all found in Geoffrey Lilburne, *The Life Between: West Coast Poems* (Adelaide: Ginninderra Press, 2020).

The poem is a simple expression of elements of the depressive experience, and by opening it up in this way, I lay it before the world and also before God. I am not asking for relief, but the writing certainly brings a way of accepting and moving beyond the pain in the experience.

Other poems are more explicitly prayerful.

On a wet day at the farm

Maybe it's my age
or perhaps the weather
but I can't help looking around
and saying, All this, so much of it
is magnificent. How does it come
to be here, whose hand made it?
There's a house, there's an orchard,
shed, hay fields, cattle yard.
Evidence of many hands.

When first we came there was nothing and
we had little, Dad and I, our bare hands,
an empty tin can, some rudimentary tools
from his back yard. What we had were dreams,
visions, hope, energy. So we worked, day after day,
not noticing that whenever we did, something
changed, something grew and remained. Now we
have all the remainders of those days, the tailings of
that labour, and like the Lord Almighty, on this wet day
I say, it is good, very good.
Blessed be.

Once again, an experience of weather outside prompts a moment of stillness, of recollection, a new kind of list emerges and it finally becomes a litany of thanks and remembrance.

In Teresa's account of prayer life as the cultivation of a garden, at the third stage of prayer, she speaks of water flowing from a river or a spring. This prayer experience is marked by delight as the soul finds that the labour is less burdensome. Teresa writes:

> The consolation, the sweetness and delight are incomparably greater than that experienced in the previous prayer. The water of grace rises up to the throat of this soul since it can no longer move forward; nor does it know how; nor can it more backwards. It would desire to enjoy the greatest glory... Nor does the soul then know what to do because it doesn't know whether to speak or to be silent, whether to laugh or to weep. This prayer is a glorious foolishness, a heavenly madness where the true wisdom is learned: and it is for the soul a most delightful way of enjoying.[11]

The freedom and delight out of which poetry arises is captured here. It is of interest that in connection with this third mode of prayer, Teresa speaks of a person who began to write poetry in this state.

> What is the soul like when it is in this state? It would want to be all tongues so as to praise the Lord. It speaks folly in a thousand holy ways, ever trying to find a means of pleasing the one who thus possesses it. I know a person who though not

---

[11] *Writings of Teresa of Avila*, pp. 22, 23.

a poet suddenly composed some deeply felt verses well expressing her pain. They were not composed by the use of intellect; rather, in order that she enjoy the glory so delightful a distress gave her, she complained of it in this way to God.[12]

In these early poems, there is a kind of exultation in the delight one feels with the objects of sense and all that lies before one. It is a kind of madness or possession by a spirit one cannot exactly identify. While for me it marked a move into a kind of poetry, for Teresa it is a sign that the relationship with God is undergoing a deepening and prayer is becoming a new kind of experience.

Prayers of a Farmer

What is the place of prayer? Where do we pray, where are we most moved to pray? Where is the space wherein our spirits can come to rest and reflect upon the divine presence? The simplistic answer is 'Well, anywhere', but that makes the dubious assumption of a featureless and homogenous space, a rather Greek and non-poetic approach. I had already discovered the importance of a monastery setting for a certain style of prayer, and began to long for my own place where my life of prayer might flourish as I saw in the monks at St Joseph's.

---

[12] *Writings*, p. 24.

When we returned to Australia in 1989, I found myself surveying rural properties for sale within reach of our home city. Of course, I wanted to fulfil what had always been my ambition, to become a farmer. Thwarted for over 30 years, it seemed the time had come. The purchase of a small hill-side property fulfilled a deep longing that reaches back to boyhood. Stock was purchased, fences and stock-yards built, and soon we had a real live little farm. But when my father retired from the work because of his age and ill-health, I continued religiously to visit the place. Set in the midst of an energetic and busy life of suburban ministry, the farm became my place of relaxation, taking stock, and indeed of prayer.

In the desire of my heart for a farm, I had no idea that it would become the place I needed to carry further my journey into prayer. Every time I went there, or spent a night, I would find myself unintentionally thanking and praising God for the gift of this place. It seemed totally undeserved and unmerited, an evidence to me of divine grace. It took years and a disastrous move interstate to pursue a career opportunity – for me to realise how vital to my life and spirit was the repose of this place, the possibility of a new entry into my relationship with God. So now my poetry and my prayer came together for me in a place where it seemed to me the presence of God was palpable.

Pilgrim's Rest

How it prospers
this little farm of mine
house quite snug
with green painted trim.

Cattle munch dry grass
The shed full of hay,
baled on a few acres
at foot of the hill.

An old ute transports
me around to inspect
water levels, animals'
progress, pilgrim journey.

In this place there is no
Slough of Despond
only green vistas to please
eye succour spirit.

Still, the desire to be a farmer and to prove it to all the world (myself principally) continued to move my mind and when the neighbour came and offered to sell me the adjoining acreage, I could see my dream taking shape. Fortunately, the asking price was beyond my means and I had to let it go. Somewhere about this time, I realised that this wasn't the point of my farm. Not exactly a prayer, but a measure of my faith journey was the new poem.

Sufficiency

It is enough
this hillside
my dog to run free
cows grow fat.

I crank up the old ute
a tour of inspection.
Overnight, nothing has moved

cattle munch hay, fires
die down, grass is damp
with early morning dew.

Naturally, I could desire more
but if the Lord is shepherd
leading into green pastures
by still waters
I shall not want.

Of course, I am blessed in having found this place. But anyone can find their place for prayer. Many would find my place isolated and lonely, too hot or too cold or not at all conducive to prayer. It is **my** place, and it is the place that enables me to continue in prayer. Roberta Bondi speaks of a special chair in her study where she practises her prayer, and Teresa speaks of her secret garden.[13] Teresa's choice of the garden imagery to describe the stages of a prayer life is surely more than coincidental. It must have been suggested by her experience of praying in a garden, an ordered but calm outdoor place where the processes of nature, of day and night, the passage of the seasons held many reminders of God's presence and providential care.

---

[13] Roberta C. Bondi tells of a journey of prayer that is informed by the Desert Fathers and Mothers. For Bondi, prayer has been a way of healing the 'wounds of the heart'. In her journey, the counsel of the desert mystics has enabled the one praying to find healing and freedom from deep seated personal wounds. See Roberta C. Bondi, *Memories of God: Reflections on a Life* (Nashville: Abingdon Press, 1995), *In Ordinary Time: Healing the Wounds of the Heart*, (Nashville: Abingdon Press, 1996) and *A Place to Pray: Reflections on the Lord's Prayer*, (Nashville: Abingdon Press, 1998).

Beyond this, it seems that a certain style of 'agrarianism' has formed my spirituality. While the farm provides a place for prayer, it is also a living metaphor of the very giftedness of life, as season follows upon season, and the cycle of life and death produces its increase. When my struggle to 'make a living' on the farm came to an end, I was able to see how much it taught me about the scale and limits of ambition. In saying that it is enough, one has reached the kind of awareness that has guided Franciscan spirituality with its embrace of the 'simple life'.[14] For me, the farm also points to a form of community, community not based on facile 'sociability' but rather upon mutuality of need and capability. In a rural community, you need good neighbours and you need in turn to be a good neighbour. As Wendell Berry would have it, these things are among the 'never-to-be official institutions that alone have the power to re-establish us in our true estate and identity'. In this way, we may be able to 'provide for the safekeeping of the small acreage of the universe that has been entrusted to us'.[15]

---

[14] Conversations with my friend Revd Peter Llewellyn enriched my understanding of the Franciscan way.

[15] Wendell Barry, 'Man and Woman in Search of Common Ground', in Norman Wirzba, *The Art of the Commonplace: The Agrarian Essays of Wendell Berry*, (Berkeley: Counterpoint, 2002), pp. 135-143.

Prayer in Ministry

As I continued in Christian ministry, my own prayer life was enriched by the experience of seeking to lead others in corporate prayer. Yet there are important differences between private and corporate prayer. What have I learnt over the years about the public ministry of prayer? Perhaps a few observations will be in order here.

In leading others, I believe it is important to find a natural rather than an 'elevated' or artificial voice, that is, a voice that is natural to the people who are to be led in prayer. What is the natural voice of prayer, especially when it comes to praise and adoration? A natural place to begin is with thanksgiving, as all people know more or less how to say thank you. The range of gifts and blessings we all enjoy are not far to seek. A practice of thanksgiving leads quite naturally into praise as we reflect together on the range of good things we enjoy at the hands of a generous God. Adoration is more difficult, and needs to arise from a deepening sense of the wonder of God linked with a sense of the closeness of the divine blessing. When confessing in public prayer, it is important to use language that is inclusive and not of a private nature.

Having said this, it is important to add that leading others in prayer is a great privilege and a considerable challenge. It requires an exercise of the imagination to put oneself into the shoes or the hearts of those with whom prayer is being offered, and, beyond that skill, in articulating the needs and longings of the pray-ers. Above all, it seems to me, it requires a steady attention on the divine nature and the divine presence.

To Whom are these prayers addressed? And what is the nature of this addressee? Losing sight of God leads to all kinds of aberrations in public prayer.

One kind of public prayer which is to be avoided is the prayer that is addressed to the human hearers and not to God. Many a preacher finds prayer an opportunity to apply the message of his or her sermon to the hearts of the believers. 'Lord, help us to rise up and put into practice the injunctions we have heard today... to be better disciples, to go out into the world in love...' etc. This is not prayer, but a kind of crypto coaching of the hearers to take up the preacher's suggestions for a better Christian life.

The subject of all our prayers is God. It takes skill and experience to keep ever before us the exalted and loving nature of God, and not to slip into addressing the congregation. It is natural, perhaps, to be more conscious of the presence of the hearers than to trust and know the presence of God, and inexperienced pray-ers will often fall into this trap. We need always to remember that in leading others in prayer, we are challenging their imaginations and their faith to know that their words are addressed to Another who is more deeply present than they themselves.

It seems to me that this kind of awareness comes only with practice of the discipline of prayer. One's leading in prayer will only be as good as one's own attention to prayer in the reality of one's own life. But, of course, one's private prayer is deepened and enriched by the exercise of prayer within the community, whether as leader or as led. If for me the sequence has been from private prayer to public praying, I'm sure for others the reverse will be true. The faith in which we are formed has always been a communal faith with communal practices, and it is good to be constantly reminded of this fact.

Ignatian Spirituality and the Dark Night

One of the many gifts of my second marriage was access to Sophia's Roman Catholic spirituality. Soon after our marriage, we joined a Christian Life Community group which met regularly for prayer in the Ignatian tradition. If the prayer of the poet and the farmer move from the head to the heart as more of a person is drawn into prayer, some old habits drop away and new ones are formed. I believe Ignatian spirituality takes us even further in this direction.

In this discipline, we are encouraged to attend to the affections of our own heart, both its consolations and its desolations. It is entirely possible for one who has moved away from the naïve prayer to believe that what goes on in one's own affective life is not a sure guide to the real state of things. Indeed, having had to deal with a mood disorder, one of my early lessons was to 'bracket out' many of my own feelings and to let my head rather than my heart determine my prayer journey.

Yet if prayer is to be an exercise of the entire person, this stance must be challenged. Like most pre-modern writers, Ignatius believed that the Spirit of God worked directly on the human heart and human consciousness. There is an immediacy of the contact of the divine presence and human feeling. As moderns, we have learned to attribute much of our conscious affect to psychological and internal factors, and to see the activity of the divine as either absent, or, at least, at one remove. But if God is at 'one remove', how do we claim the divine presence at all?

It seems that Ignatian spirituality encourages us to think in terms of emerging dispositions and settled convictions. Thus a 'consolation' is not an immediate feeling of joy or uplift, but rather an emerging disposition of joy as we contemplate over time a certain course of action or event. Likewise, a desolation is not a momentary feeling of disappointment so much as a settled sense that a certain course or event is not properly rewarding. Attention to our dispositions enables us to move to prayer that is more truly affective, and involves as much listening and giving attention as it does to directing words and intentions out into the world.

Yet in this journey, there is still the 'dark night of the soul'. For me, the experience of darkness took, first, the form of a crippling depression. In the earliest days of my prayer life, I had the belief that my subjective states were brought about by some direct action of God on my soul or spirit. Not so much in the descent of darkness for which I wholly blamed myself but the lifting of the darkness, the access of light and the relief of my anxiety symptoms. I spoke most freely and joyfully of God's 'deliverance' from my inbuilt failings.

As my psychological understanding grew, I came to realise that there was a certain disconnect or distance between my subjective states and the will and activity of God. I realised I needed to gain an 'objective' sense of my own feelings, and to find God somewhat outside and beyond them. For the practical atheist I confess to be, this was not such a difficult move, as it might have been for John or Teresa! It simply meant that I pushed my God concept further up into the distant heavens of transcendence. I did not need to surrender my conviction about the sovereignty of God, but merely to distance the divine activity from my own subjective states.

But then what would be the point of prayer? If God were so distant, could there persist a sense of an attending divine presence in any realistic sense? I think for a long time, I gave up on the practice of prayer: not only did it not make a difference, at times it was positively harmful as it seemed to increase anxiety and make one even more conscious of one's wretchedness. It was better to talk to flesh and blood than to this distant God. But then there emerges a new kind of dissonance: one believes in prayer and the sovereign purpose of God, but one does not practise. A kind of Deistic faith and practice is the result, and certainly something less than Christian.

It is perhaps fairly straightforward to live as a Christian believer but to cease the practice of personal prayer. I think many clergy find themselves living this way. They do the work of God *for him*, so there is no need to actually pray *to him*, or relate *with him*! But there is a dissonance which will trouble the reflective soul. There is, in fact, a real opening here to a kind of idolatry, in which an image of God or of the self is raised in place of the living God. Idolatry is a real danger in the lives of many well informed and educated Christians who fondly imagine that have moved beyond the piety of their youth. Prayer – as I have been at pains to point out – is not an expression of some piety, it is the breath of the soul in the divine atmosphere of adult life.

Ignatian practice offer a way to check on some of these dangers. It calls for a daily *examen*, a practice like a nightly review of the day, dwelling particularly on experiences of desolation and consolation. In this mode of reflection, one is not directly attributing every feeling with divine presence, but rather identifying particular experiences that stand out as bringing either sorrow or joy, pain or pleasure.

We review the events both objective and subjective of the day, with a view to saying wherein we sensed a consolation of spirit, and wherein our spirit was desolated. While not directly attributing our feelings and emotions to divine causation, we seek to discern the working of God in these deeply subjective experiences. We give thanks for the moments of consolation, we ponder the moments of desolation and seek to discern through them the working of a divine purpose in our lives. We come back to our experience and to prayer, and seek to find new ways of discerning the working of God in all things.

Theological Enlightenment

In the Ignatian framework, depressive episodes count as real desolation, and the relief of depression as a moment of consolation. Prayer in and around these moments assumes a new presence of the divine in our life of prayer. God again draws near and the person praying is encouraged to know that the divine is not at all distant from all things, including the matters of the human heart and the human consciousness. In this way, a modest recovery of the experiential aspect of prayer is possible, and is enhanced. In its way, this offers a form of theological enrichment.

Indeed, it is through depressive episodes that one gains a new discernment as to how it might be that there is divine leading even in depression. I realise that this is still a far cry from John's view of the dark night – as evidence of God's obscure working in the human soul – but it seems to me it offers us a glimpse of a way that depression might be moved away from our 'pathology' diagnosis to something more positive in the journey of a Christian soul. Depression leads to a deepening of consciousness, both of the self and its limits and of the divine in its interaction with the human person.

While the first theological impulse of my growing understanding of depression was to see God as higher in the heavens, that is, to place God at some remove from the progression of my subjective states, the prayer of patient waiting saw a God who was desiring to draw closer, in relief and healing. The joy that so suddenly disappeared with the onset of my depressions was now waiting in the wings to re-emerge in blessing. The distant and seemingly unwilling God of my adolescent prayer was now seen more as one whose times could not be predetermined or controlled, the gracious One upon whom I needed to wait.

Here the image Henri Nouwen employs of the 'wounded healer' informed my perception of Jesus and of the God of Jesus. This healer is not removed into the highest heavens but walks the road beside us. I was slow to fully grasp the powerful theology of this perception, but gradually it became clearer to me in the days when joy returned. This theological shift already points in the direction of understanding God as Holy Trinity.

There had been 'trinitarian' hints in my theological understanding, in my experience of Jesus as my Lord in conversion days, and later in my struggle over the baptism of the Holy spirit. But these indications had been largely eliminated by my over-riding sense of God as a strict and somewhat demanding Parent figure. It is easy to assimilate the experience of Jesus and the Spirit into a sense of the character of the transcendent One. Yet as I moved to see God in more compassionate and nurturing terms, I reflected on the trinitarian nature of God, allowing the character of the Son and the Spirit to transform the sense of God's very being.

To understand God as love in relationship, or as Karl Barth has it, the One who loves in freedom, opens the way for a more nuanced and rich understanding of God as Father, Son and Holy Spirit. The anxieties and jeopardies of the human lot are hereby opened to a vision of God as the One able to reach down to the depths and to enter into the anguish of human suffering. With such an understanding, the anxious and depressed person is enabled to draw near to God in hope and patience. Rather than union with the transcendent God, this trinitarian view calls us to a relationship with God who is defined as relationship of Father, Son and Spirit.

4

Journey's End

All human experience is bounded and, as we age, we know there is an end in sight. Try as we might, we cannot avoid thoughts about that end and what journeys will cease with it. We are taught to see death as the enemy we must fear, but the poets point us to another possibility. Emily Dickinson captures this perfectly in her poem.

> Because I could not stop for Death,
> He kindly stopped for me;
> The carriage held but just ourselves
> And Immortality.[16]

In the end, death may be a kindness, a friend rather than the enemy we dreaded.

But if in our prayer, we have grown to seek and to know the presence of the divine Love, then the thought of death may mean no cessation, but more like a translation into a new Presence. Of course, we do not know and can only conjecture. Religious faith tries to plumb the depths with fanciful images and narrative, but we all must face this reality with open minds. Theodore Roethke speaks of a kind of 'waking'.

---

[16] Emily Dickinson, *Selected Poems and Letters of Emily Dickinson*, edited by Robert N. Linscott (New York: Doubleday Anchor Books, 1959) p. 151.

The Waking

I wake to sleep and take my waking slow.
I feel my fate in what I cannot fear.
I learn by going where I have to go.

We think by feeling, what is there to know?
I hear my being dance from ear to ear.
I wake to sleep and take my waking slow.

Of those so close beside me which are you?
God bless the Ground! I shall walk softly there
and learn by going where I have to go.

Light takes the Tree, but who can tell us how?
The lowly worm climbs up a winding stair.
I wake to sleep and take my waking slow.

Great Nature has another thing to do
To you and me, so take the lively air,
And lovely, learn by going where to go.

This shaking keeps me steady, I should know.
What falls away is always. And is near.
I wake to sleep and take my waking slow.
I learn by going where I have to go.[17]

It is indeed a reality that we will only learn as we 'have to go'. Thoughts such as these led me to write a little poem in support of death.

---

[17] Theodore Roethke, *The Collected Poems of Theodore Roethke* (Garden City, New York: Anchor Books, 1975), p. 104.

In Support of Death

The nearer I come to my demise
the more I fear that of others,
and the less my own.

My children, my dear wife,
even my beloved pet
I most dread.

It's inevitable –
with so many now gone
perhaps an act of belated solidarity
to join them in that other realm.

Assuming, of course, there is another realm,
and a them to join, all of which
is unknown at this point.

Call me morbid, if you wish,
or just plain selfish.
I like to go first.

What we know is that our words will fall away, and our little poems die on the page, but the life of prayer, the laying out of our entire lives in the divine presence may only cease to be an exercise and become our reality.

When Teresa writes about the fourth and final stage of prayer, the prayer of union, she does so with a degree of diffidence. If a contemplative from the age of faith writes in this way, how much more a secular man writing in the god-less 21st century! It seems that for Teresa, the stage of union is marked by a degree of obscurity.

The prayer is not experienced as work but as glory. In this fourth water, the soul isn't in possession of its senses, but it rejoices without knowing what it is rejoicing in. It understands that it is enjoying a good in which are gathered all goods, but this good is incomprehensible.

This prayer of union is accompanied by a loss of all the senses, in what she calls a 'kind of swoon'.

How this prayer they call union comes about and what it is, I don't know how to explain. Neither do I understand what the mind is; nor do I know how it differs from the soul or the spirit... The Lord spoke these words to me; 'It (the soul) detaches itself from everything, daughter, so as to abide more in me. It is no longer the soul that lives but I. Since it cannot comprehend what it understands, there is an understanding by not understanding'. In this prayer, all the faculties fail and they are so suspended that in no way... does one think they are working... The intellect, if it understands, doesn't know how it understands.[18]

I can lay no claim to understanding this mystery, nor to have ever experienced it. But it does sound like a kind of death, the end of sensory experience as such. As I think about the end of this life's journey and what lies beyond, this vision

---

[18] *Writings of Teresa of Avila*, pp. 27-30.

of a prayer of union fills me with a kind of joyful hope. It is surely something for even lost secular souls to long for. In the end, the showers of blessing may be without end.

5

What is Prayer?

Towards a definition

I thank you, my reader, for journeying with me in this little narrative. At the outset, I argued that the place to begin was not a definition of prayer but rather with a lived experience. Now that I've revealed something of my unremarkable experience of prayer, it is time to fulfil the promise of reaching a definition!

We have seen prayer as a verbal discipline, a matter of a routine with lists and all manner of needs enumerated. But that discipline only took us so far; so, in changed circumstances, the need of prayer was more for silence and recollection. Gradually, we learn that prayer is not something we do with our minds alone, but is an exercise of the body. At times, it might be appropriate to bow in silence, at other times it might be better to walk. In the depth of depression we find that words themselves become hollow, and that prayer as 'waiting in hope' is a far better way to go.

The forming of words, sentences, petitions can also become the voicing of a poetic voice. Claiming and exercising the poetic voice is a way of laying a heart and mind open to the world, open to God. We need not resist the attraction of poetry as if it would take us away from God. It leads, I believe, to a deeper immersion in the divine.

Amongst the Trappists, we discovered that prayer can be song and that the setting of the song is as important as the tune or even the words. As a silent order, the monks at St Joseph's also knew of prayer as a silent discipline. Few of us are called to monastic orders, but for those on the 'outside' the place of prayer is very important, and can be as specific as the location of Spencer, Massachusetts.

So might prayer best be defined as the opening of a soul – a whole soul, including a body located in space and time – to the loving and sustaining divine Presence? Rather than 'talking to God', such a definition makes way for the prayer of silence, of poetry, of song. When we say 'soul' we do not mean to separate off the 'spiritual' part of ourselves, for we know that while we have many aspects or sides, real prayer involves the whole of ourselves in a total act of self-giving. As we learn to open all aspects of the lives we are given back to the Giver, we begin, however, fitfully along the great journey of prayer.

Prayer is a journey, and that journey has some discernible stages. While its beginnings might be quite spontaneous, as the new Christian delights to open their heart to God, it soon becomes something of a discipline, requiring work and concentration of intellect. For a time, the delight might be lost, the joy eclipsed, but from time to time they return. For the seasoned pray-er, the balance of work and gift, of discipline and joy may shift from time to time. But there is no season without its reward, and although there may be periods of acute darkness, the light of the divine presence has a habit of breaking through. Praying with others, leading a congregation or community in prayer, adds dimensions to the personal experience of prayer.

However much one seeks a union with God, this consummation seems to be denied to most mortals, especially those living in a secular age. But for those who face death with faith, this blessed hope may be just what the soul longs for in illness and physical decline. Faith continues to hope, hope continues to exercise faith, and the sum of these things is a loving joy of the final stage of the journey. Perhaps we wake to sleep, and learn by going where we have to go.

Prayer as Transformative

We have glimpsed aspects of the prayer journey of the medieval saints, Teresa and John. For John and Teresa, the life of prayer is a journey into union with God. In John's account, this inevitably leads to the 'dark night' when the human is purged of all the attachments and affections that hold it to this life. Founded in a psychological dualism between the flesh and the spirit, or the body and the soul, this understanding is no longer in keeping with contemporary ways of understanding the human person. Yet in medieval psychology this purgation is at its heart a movement of transformation, and I believe that this understanding needs to be recaptured in our modern setting.

In a series of remarkable books, Roberta C. Bondi, professor emerita at the Candler School of Theology in Emory University, tells of her life journey with prayer.[19] In important ways, I believe, Bondi's writing may point us to a new way of approaching the idea of 'transformation through prayer' we have encountered in one form in Teresa and John.

Describing her life's journey from Kentucky to Oxford to Atlanta, Bondi relates her accompanying struggle with inherited notions both of the self and of God. The Southern Baptist preachers of her childhood instilled in her a fear of an angry God who punished his Son for the sins of the whole world, including the sins of her unhappy childhood. In Seminary, however, Bondi came to a more rational understanding of God and the Christian faith, which, while bringing temporary comfort, never fully addressed the angry God of the old-style evangelists. It was reading a homily from Philoxenus of Mabbug in the Bodleian Library at Oxford that opened her heart and mind to a new vision of God.

> God the Father is gentle and makes allowances?
> God the Father especially loves the castoffs?
> What would this mean, if this really were true?
> Was God really uninterested in sin? Could God
> the Father expect *less* of me than my human
> father? Could God the Father *want* and even *like*
> women the church I knew rejected? I did not
> know the answers to these questions, but I knew

---

[19] Roberta C. Bondi, *Memories of God: Theological Reflections of a Life* (Nashville: Abingdon Press, 1995).

the somehow these people who lived nearly a
millennium and a half ago had spoken to me
directly out of their own love, and of God's love
for me.[20]

This discovery was the beginning of a long process
of healing that was enabled by her life of prayer. Bondi
details steps along the way to wholeness, a journey centred
in her habit of daily prayer. There were many issues to
confront, issues which in some contexts would have been
the occasion for psychological therapy and techniques of
recaptured memory. By making these struggles the sites for
her prayer, Bondi is able to tell of a life-long process in which
the wounds of her heart were healed.

Once begun, I was on a journey into a nearly
unknown territory. Painfully, over a matter of
years, with the monastic teachers' help, I was able
to lay aside my modern assumptions about prayer.
I gave up the idea that prayer is about finding
peace, or about accepting whatever happens in
life, no matter how tragic, as the will of God.
I abandoned the notion that prayer is basically
verbal petition and praise, and came to see that
prayer is a sharing of the whole self and an entire
life with God.[21]

---

[20] Bondi, *Memories*, p. 31.
[21] Bondi, *Memories*, pp. 33, 34.

In giving up modern assumptions about prayer, Bondi moves closer to the understanding of the Desert Fathers and Mothers that prayer is more like 'warfare to the end'. Her unhelpful images of God the Father had to be worked through in prayer, so she resolved to use only the 'Father' name for God for a season of prayer, until the new understanding of her mind reached the heart. Healing this relationship lead also to a healing in her actual relations with her earthly father.

Rather than needing to be 'purged' of all earthly attachments, this healing prayer led to all kinds of changes in the pray-ers heart and mind. Recapturing the image of herself as female in the image of God also took a slow process of praying self-acceptance and renewing understanding of the love of God. Finally, the cross itself needed a new understanding, if it was to move out of the sin-punishment frame of early versions of the atonement. Bondi describes how for a while she lost any sense of the meaning of the crucifixion, and one Easter prayed to God.

> I have failed in everything you have given me to do. I have tried so hard to be a good mother. With my whole heart I have wanted to love my children enough to keep them safe and happy. I have suffered with them and for them. I have begged you to help me to love them well and in the right way, but the harder I try the more I worry. There must be something essential about Christianity I am missing, something I can't see. I give up. If there is something you want me to

know, you must find me yourself to tell me. I can
try no longer, and I can look no longer. I give up.
I absolutely give up.[22]

Having given up, she rediscovered the meaning of the
resurrection in the Roman Catholic eucharistic prayers for
Easter: 'The joy of the Resurrection renews the whole world'.
The words rang true and filled her heart with an untold
relief and happiness. The mystery of the cross lies not in a
sacrificial death so much as in a triumphant rising to new
life, the opening of joy for every believer, and, indeed, for the
whole world. The story of how these theological realisations
gradually transformed her life through prayer is wonderfully
told in this series of books.

Being in God

We may finally trace the progression of prayer in the
following way. For many of us, prayer begins as an addition
to our normal lives. For some reason, it might be through a
conversion experience, or a different kind of crisis, that we
are drawn to start praying. In this exercise of prayer, we find
some joy and something of a burden. For some – many, I fear –
the burden soon outweighs the joy, and they give up praying
at all. The addition is subtracted! For others, however, the
discipline of prayer kicks in and they persist to pray. Perhaps

---

[22] Bondi, *Memories*, p. 169.

they are reading Paul's advice to 'pray without ceasing' or perhaps the crises of their lives multiply. They find themselves pouring out their hearts to God in earnest supplication.

But we are all in process; and what does this prayer for rescue become in their lives? Again, when the crises of life pass for a while, perhaps they give up praying altogether, or perhaps they make the transition to prayers of thanksgiving, for relief received and new joy opening. Then the discipline of prayer begins to give way to a habit of prayer, a habit that begins to form or, should we say, re-form one's life. For as Bondi has taught so clearly, this habit opens the way for transformation of a person.

Life is long and varied, and as we go through the various changes that come to us, prayer may continue and even increase in our lives, or it may slowly drop out. For some, a situation of grief or great loss leads us to give up or to blame God for the misfortune that has stuck us. I am stressing this point – that there are many ways in which we tend to give up on prayer – because I see so many who do give up praying as they mature, or as their lives settle into a pattern of adulthood and old age. To pray without ceasing is not the usual pattern of life these days, and I wish to sound my voice in saying that this is a great loss to persons and to communities. Here is surely a central teaching of Jesus to keep on asking so that we may receive in God's good time. Persistence is the great lesson of his teaching and example.

For the ones who persist, there is a further transition. While prayer starts out as something we do, if we learn the lesson of continuing in prayer, it becomes eventually something we are. Rather than an added activity to our lives, prayer becomes our very being. This, it seems to me, is the promise of praying without ceasing, that our very lives become a prayer, a gesture towards God that is at once a thanksgiving and a supplication, a confession of failure and a celebration of joy and blessing. I do not expect that it will ever cease for me to be, at times a discipline and something I do, but as I continue in the life of prayer, I find increasingly that it is more about who I am than what I do. I believe it could be so also for you.

Whilst this may seem to be something less than the medieval goal of 'union with God', I wonder if in this age so marked by a loss of the sense of God – my own functional atheism – it might be more helpful to think in terms of our very selves becoming a prayer. Of course, as our imaginations are recharged in a lifetime of prayer, this realisation can also be seen as a union of the self with the divine, a growing of the Christ in us through the working of the Holy Spirit. I have not focused explicitly on the Triunity of God in this narrative, but such an understanding really undergirds all that I have thought and said about prayer. If it is the Spirit who enables us to pray in the first place, it is the call of Christ to prayer that motivate and energises our journey. To be drawn into the relations of Father, Son and Holy Spirit is the final goal and prize of a life of prayer.

A Treasury of Prayers

Here are some prayers that put into words the hopes and fears of my heart. I have returned to these prayers frequently, in differing times and circumstances, and, after even repeated praying, they still seem to hold true. The first is a prayer I discovered early in my prayer journey that seemed to sum up my hopes for a Sunday, before I entered ministry. The covenant-making prayer comes from the same period, from my early worship experience in the Methodist Church.

Bruce Prewer gave us many fine litanies for use in worship and this is a favourite of mine. Doug Mackenzie's prayer is a good Uniting Church prayer, while the litany from Lucien Deiss I find particularly moving in the way it moves from unfounded to realistic hope. I find that Leunig recalls us to matters we don't often think to pray about. The next two prayers come from my pastoral ministry in a rural Western Australian congregation. We used a form of the Ignatian prayer in my Boy Scout days, and I choose it to close this brief selection.

A Sunday Prayer,
John Baillie

O God, I crave Thy blessing upon this day of rest and refreshment. Let me rejoice today in Thy worship and find gladness in singing of thy praises. Forbid, I beseech Thee, that only my body should be refreshed today, and not my spirit. Give me grace for such an act of self-recollection as may again bring together the scattered forces of my soul. Enable me to step aside for a little while from the busy life of common days and take thought about its meaning and its end. May Jesus Christ be today the companion of my thoughts, so that His divine manhood may more and more take root within my soul. May He be in me and I in Him, even as Thou wert in Him and through Him mayest be in me and I at rest in Thee.

O Thou who art the Source and Ground of all truth, Thou Light of lights, who has opened the minds of men to discern the things that are, guide me today, I beseech Thee, in my hours of reading. Give me grace to choose the right books and to read them in the right way. Give me wisdom to abstain as well as to persevere. Let the Bible have proper place; and grant that as I read I may be alive to the stirrings of Thy Holy Spirit in my soul.

I pray, O God, for all human hearts that today are lifted up to Thee in earnest desire, and for every group of men and women who are met together to praise and magnify Thy name. Whatever be their mode of worship, be graciously pleased to accept their humble offices of prayer and praise, and lead them unto life eternal, through Jesus Christ our Lord. Amen.[23]

At Your Coming,

Bruce Prewer

1. Where two or three gather
together in your name,
yet become self-satisfied
exclusive and self-serving:

At dusk or at daybreak,
midnight or midday,
wake us at your coming.

2. Behind the soul's locked doors,
listening to our own wants,
protecting our privileges,
suspicious of your knock:

---

[23] John Baillie, *A Diary of Private Prayer* (London, Toronto: Geoffrey Cumberlege, Oxford University Press, 1936, 1953), p. 133.

At dusk or at daybreak,
midnight or midday,
wake us at your coming.

3. In the breaking of bread,
repeated so frequently
that familiarity had bred
nonchalance and loss of wonder:

At dusk or at daybreak,
midnight or midday,
wake us at your coming.

4. Among the hungry and thirsty,
homeless and deserted,
street kids and refugees,
and the poor always with us:

At dusk or at daybreak,
midnight or midday,
wake us at your coming.

5. On the road to the world's end,
witnessing to your name,
sure of our mission,
too sure of our dogmas:

At dusk or at daybreak,
midnight or midday,
wake us at your coming.

6. On the day of consummations,
when all in heaven and earth
will be brought into unity
and God will be all in all:

At dusk or at daybreak...
midnight or midday,
wake us at your coming.[24]

Prayer of Kevin Hart

O come, in any way you want,
In morning sunlight fooling in the leaves
Or in thick bouts of rain that soak my head.

Because of what the darkness said

Or come, though far too slowly for my eye to see,
Like a dark hair that fades to gray

Come with the wind that wraps my house

Or winter light that slants upon a page

Because the beast is stirring in its cage

---

[24] Bruce D. Prewer, *More Australian Psalms*, (Adelaide, South Australia, 1996), p. 120.

Or come in raw and ragged smells
Of gum leaves dangling down at noon
Or in the undertow of love
When she's away

Because a night creeps through the day

Come as you used to, years ago
When I first fell for you

In the deep calm of an autumn morning
Beginning with the cooing of a dove

Because of love, the lightest love

Or if that's not your way these days
Because of me, because
Of something dead in me,
Come like a jagged knife into my gut

Because your touch will surely cut

Come any way you want

But come[25]

[25] Kevin Hart, *Young Rain* (Artarmon, NSW; Giramondo Publishing Co., 2008), pp. 17, 18

Covenant Making Prayer

Beloved in Christ
let us again claim this covenant for ourselves,
and take the yoke of Christ upon us.

To take this yoke upon us again means we are content
that he appoint us our place and work,
and that he himself be our reward.

Christ has many services to be done:
some are easy, others are difficult;
some bring honour, others bring reproach:
some are suitable to our natural inclinations
and material interests,
others are contrary to both.
In some we may please Christ and please ourselves;
in others we cannot please Christ
except by denying ourselves.
Yet the power to do all these things
is given us in Christ, who strengthens us.

Therefore let us make this covenant with God our own,
trusting in the eternal promises
and relying on divine grace.

> I am no longer my own, but yours.
> Put me to what you will,
> rank me with whom you will;
> put me to doing, put me to suffering;

let me be employed for you or laid aside for you;
exalted for you or brought low for you;
let me be full, let me be empty;
let me have all things, let me have nothing;
I freely and wholeheartedly yield all things
to your pleasure and disposal.

And now, glorious and blessed God,
Father, Son and Holy Spirit,
you are mine and I am yours,
to the glory and praise of your name. Amen.[26]

A Rolling Brown Land,
Douglas McKenzie

Lord God,
your Spirit has moved over the face of Australia
and formed from its dust a rolling brown land.
Your Spirit has moved over its warm tropical waters
and created a rich variety of life.
Your Spirit has moved in the lives
of men, women and children
and given them, from the dreamtime,
an affinity with their lands and waters.
Your Spirit has moved in pilgrim people
and brought them to a place of freedom and plenty.
Your Spirit moves still today
in sprawling, high-rise cities,

---

[26] *Uniting in Worship: Peoples Book* (Melbourne: Uniting Church Press, 1988), pp. 49, 50.

in the vast distances of the outback,
and in the ethnic diversity of the Australian people.

Lord God,
in the midst of this varied huddle of humanity
you have set your church.
Give us, the people you have so richly blessed,
a commitment to justice and peace for all nations;
and a vision of righteousness
and equality for all people in our country.
Help us look beyond our far horizons
to see our neighbours in their many guises,
so that we may be mutually enriched by our differences.
And may our love and compassion for all people on earth
be as wide and varied as our land
and as constant as the grace of our Lord, Jesus Christ. Amen.

The Revd Douglas McKenzie.[27]

Those Trusting in You,
Lucien Deiss

For the husband or the wife
who awaits the return of one who has left
and will never return,
    we pray to you, Lord.
Those trusting in you, O Lord, will never be deceived.

---

[27] *Uniting in Worship: People's Book,* p. 240.

For parents
awaiting the return of a child
who will never return,
    we pray to you, Lord.
Those trusting in you, O Lord, will never be deceived.

For those who are in prison
awaiting their return home
though they will never return,
    we pray to you, Lord.
Those trusting in you, O Lord, will never be deceived.

For those who are sick
and await the return of their health
which will never return,
    we pray to you, Lord.
Those trusting in you, O Lord, will never be deceived.

For those who are yearning to die
yet see no end to their suffering,
    we pray to you, Lord.
Those trusting in you, O Lord, will never be deceived.

For the people of Israel
who are still awaiting the Saviour
because, in Jesus, they see not his presence,
    we pray to you, Lord.
Those trusting in you, O Lord, will never be deceived.

For those who are no longer waiting for anything
who do not even know there is a Savior to hope for,
  we pray to you, Lord.
Those trusting in you, O Lord, will never be deceived.

Lord, God of all trust,
remember your kindness,
remember your love.

Do not deceive, Lord,
those whom life has always deceived
and whose hope is only in you.
Keep them in the joy of your love.
O you, God of all wonders,
who alone can grant our desires
beyond even hope.[28]

A Prayer of Leunig

God, give us rain when we expect sun.
Give us music when we expect trouble.
Give us tears when we expect breakfast.
Give us dreams when we expect a storm.
Give us a stray dog when we expect congratulations.
God play with us, turn us sideways, and around.
Amen.[29]

---

[28] Lucien Deiss, *Come Lord Jesus: Biblical Prayers with Psalms and Scripture Readings*, (World Library Publications, 1981)

[29] Michael Leunig, *A Common Prayer* (Sydney: HarperCollins, 1990)

A Prayer of Commitment,
Ignatius Loyola

Teach us, good Lord,
to serve you as you deserve,
to give, and not to count the cost;
to fight, and not to heed the wounds;
to toil, and not to seek for rest,
to labour, and not to ask for any reward,
except that of knowing that we do your holy will,
through Jesus Christ our Lord. Amen.

St Ignatius Loyola